# Georgia:
# The Debtors Colony

Mitchell Lane
PUBLISHERS

P.O. Box 196 • Hockessin, Delaware 19707

# Titles in the Series

# Georgia:
# The Debtors Colony

Susan Sales Harkins and
William H. Harkins

Copyright © 2007 by Mitchell Lane Publishers, Inc. All rights reserved. No part of this book may be reproduced without written permission from the publisher. Printed and bound in the United States of America.

Printing    1    2    3    4    5    6    7    8    9

Library of Congress Cataloging-in-Publication Data
Harkins, Susan Sales.
  Georgia : the debtors colony / by Susan Sales Harkins and William H. Harkins.
      p. cm.—(Building America)
  Includes bibliographical references and index.
  ISBN 1-58415-465-9 (library bound)
  1. Georgia—History—Colonial period, ca. 1600–1775—Juvenile literature.
I. Harkins, William H. II. Title. III. Building America (Hockessin, Del.)
F289.H3 2007
975.8'02—dc22

                                                                    2006006096

ISBN-10:1-58415-465-9                          ISBN-13: 9781584154655

**ABOUT THE AUTHORS: Susan and Bill Harkins** live in Kentucky, where they enjoy writing together for children. Susan has written many books for adults and children. Bill is a history buff. In addition to writing, he is a member of the National Guard.

**PHOTO CREDITS:** Cover, pp. 1, 3—North Wind; p. 6—Getty Images; p. 12—Henry Francis du Pont Winterthur Museum; pp. 14, 27, 36—Library of Congress; p. 18—Smithsonian Institute; pp. 20, 22, 30, 38, 39, 40—Georgia Historical Society.

**PUBLISHER'S NOTE:** This story is based on the authors' extensive research, which they believe to be accurate. Documentation of such research is contained on page 46.

    The internet sites referenced herein were active as of the publication date. Due to the fleeting nature of some web sites, we cannot guarantee they will all be active when you are reading this book.

                                                                    PLB

# Contents

*For Your Information

*As a young man, James Oglethorpe led the ambitious expedition to found Georgia. He governed the colony according to the Trustees' rules, and for his trouble, he received nothing. He wasn't allowed to own land or profit from the venture in any way.*

Chapter

# 1

## The Promise of Georgia

In 1728, Robert Castell, a well-known architect, languished in an English prison.[1] He wasn't a violent criminal—a thief or a murderer. His crime was bankruptcy. When he couldn't pay his creditors, prison became his home. For a while, Castell was a bit luckier than most of his cell mates. For a few coins, the warden occasionally sent Castell clean clothes, fresh water, and a decent meal.

Then Castell ran out of money. The warden didn't know whether Castell was telling the truth or not. To scare him into handing over any money he might still have, the warden threatened to move him to an area of the prison infested with the smallpox virus, which meant certain death for Castell.

About that time, James Edward Oglethorpe found Castell in prison. Oglethorpe was touring the prison with a committee charged with exposing prison corruption.

The two men knew each other, and Oglethorpe was aghast to find his friend living in the prison's squalid conditions. Castell pleaded with Oglethorpe to help—Castell knew he would die if the warden moved him.

When Castell was unable to pay the warden's bribe, the warden made good on his threat and moved him. The architect died that year of smallpox, still a prisoner in Fleet Prison. Sparked by grief and anger, Oglethorpe included Castell's story in his report to England's House of Commons.[2] It was too late to help his friend, but the report had a huge impact on England.

Oglethorpe exposed more than just inmates starving in dank, dark dungeons. Everyone knew prison conditions were harsh. The report exposed the caretakers, who heaped the bodies of dead prisoners and left them for months to decompose, instead of disposing of them properly. Finding piles of rotting corpses was bad enough, but the real problem was that often, the caretakers left live prisoners chained to the dead bodies. Trapped prisoners slept, ate, and relieved themselves in the same spot while watching rats and time devour the flesh of the corpse chained to their leg.

Besides the depravity with which the wardens and guards treated the prisoners, living conditions were abominable. There was no heat or light. Sick prisoners suffered on the cold damp floor until they died, often alone in the dark. Most prisoners considered the sick lucky because they died quicker. Slowly starving to death was much worse.

At Marshalsea Prison, inmates slept in layers. Sometimes inmates on the bottom suffocated. There, the committee also found debtors chained to dead, decomposing bodies. With no personal sanitation in the prison, the prisoners relieved themselves in their cells. Between the decomposing corpses and the human waste, the stench was unbearable.

King's Bench Prison was no better. Caretakers tortured the prisoners, most of whom were debtors, not violent criminals. England's society was either ignorant of the abuse or didn't care. During the eighteenth century, London was divided by class. A person was either wealthy and powerful or was poor and insignificant. If a person was a debtor, meaning he couldn't pay his debts, he was nothing.

Not all debtors went to prison, but an average of 4,000 did go to prison each year. They stayed there until they could pay their debts. In prison, with no means of making money, a debtor's only hope was that

*Debtors in Fleet Prison call out to passersby. Prison conditions in seventeenth-century England were deplorable and Fleet Prison was one of the worst. Robert Castell, an acquaintance of James Oglethorpe's, died in the infamous Fleet Prison for no other crime than being poor. His death motivated Oglethorpe to challenge Parliament to reform the prison system.*

someone outside the prison—a family member or a friend—would pay the debt. Most debtors died in prison.

Oglethorpe deplored the system. His report was the needed catalyst for change. Jailers appeared before judges to account for their crimes, and courts released thousands of debtors from prison. In 1730, Parliament passed the Debtors Act, which protected debtors. Creditors still had the right to send someone to jail, but the debtor had twenty-four hours to raise the money. Jail conditions improved a bit, and bribery became a crime.

Prison reforms were necessary, but the consequence of reform was that London's streets became filled with unemployed debtors. London was a harsh place for the poor, who sloshed through the wet, muddy, garbage-filled streets, breathing the thick, black fog from the coal fires that warmed the city's homes and shops. They shared crowded rooms, apartments, and basements. Food was meager and irregular. Even those with jobs were often just a few meals away from debtors prison. Releasing thousands of debtors from prison increased London's already high unemployment rate and its severe poverty.

Talk of a new colony south of the Carolinas in America had been ongoing for years. In 1717, Sir Robert Montgomery proposed the idea in *A Discourse Concerning the Designed Establishment of a New Colony to the South of Carolina, in the Most Delightful Country of the Universe*. Oglethorpe saw the colony as an opportunity for London's poor. In fact, when King George II finally granted a charter to establish the new colony in 1732, Oglethorpe volunteered to lead the settlers himself and at his own expense.

Georgia, named for King George II, wasn't just a panacea for the poor—far from it. England, Spain, and France all claimed the land south of South Carolina and north of Florida. Many called the territory the Debatable Lands because so many, including the settlers in South Carolina and the American Indians who lived there, claimed it as their own. That unsettled territory left the English colonies north of it vulnerable to attack. Georgia would serve as a protective buffer for England's southern colonial frontier from the Spanish in Florida and the French to the west.

The Spanish were the greatest threat to the colonies. Nor did it help that the French did a good job of keeping the Indians angry with the English and ready to fight. A settled colony south of the Savannah River would secure South Carolina and, subsequently, all of the northern English colonies. (The river took its name from *Savannah*, the Shawnee Indians' word for their people.)

On July 20, 1732, the Trustees of the new Georgia Charter, which included Oglethorpe, met to create a smaller group called the Common Council. The council had two important jobs. First, its members must advertise settlement in the new colony. Second, they had to select the colonists.

Oglethorpe was a talented publicist, and in his capable hands, *Georgia* became a household word. Pamphlets and articles about the colony touted Georgia as a paradise. None of the Trustees had actually been to the colony, but they believed in the project. They knew Georgia could provide a better life for some of London's wretched poor. Their altruistic motives may have helped them oversell the colony, but their intentions seemed to have been honorable.[3] Londoners were excited—Georgia was the opportunity of a lifetime for the poor.

In reality, the charter was full of contradictions. The colonists had all the rights of Englishmen, but in Georgia, they would have no voice in their local government. The charter guaranteed freedom of religion, as long as the religion wasn't Roman Catholicism or Judaism.

The poor didn't quibble about government or religion. They wanted the land and the opportunities that went with it. Many wanted to go, but only a few did. The Trustees knew that the colony's success depended on its colonists. All applicants had to be debt-free. That meant either they had no debts or they had to receive permission from their creditors to leave England. In addition, no man could abandon his family in England.

The Georgia adventure was a lifetime commitment for the colonists, so the committee accepted only the most responsible and ambitious applicants. Thirty-five men and their families made the first voyage—that was all the Trustees could afford to send.

The Trustees paid passage for the poor from funds raised by the charter. Colonists received a land grant of fifty acres, seeds, tools, and a year's worth of provisions. Anyone able to pay his own way received a larger land grant. Restrictions kept the colonists from owning the land outright: Only a male heir could inherit the land and no colonist could sell or mortgage his land.

Each colonist agreed to defend the new colony using arms and ammunition provided by the Trustees. In addition, each colonist agreed to stay in the colony for at least three years.

Initially, settlers had no voice in the colonial government. The Trustees maintained complete control through Oglethorpe, who administered the colony. However, the charter restricted the Trustees as well. No Trustee could own land in Georgia, nor could he profit from any trade. The role of Trustee was strictly one of a benevolent overseer.[4]

Government wasn't all the Trustees controlled. A lot of planning went into the colony, and the Trustees determined what the colonists would grow and produce. They were convinced that the land and

Oglethorpe (in black, center) addresses the Georgia Trustees and a group of Creek Indians in 1734. The Creek had traveled to London for this meeting. The Trustees were well-meaning and charitable, but they didn't know much about Georgia.

climate were perfect for raising silkworms. Establishing a silk industry in an American colony would be an economic coup for England. Eventually, the Trustees required each colonist to plant white mulberry trees as they cleared the land. Silkworms would eat the white mulberry leaves. From the silkworms, the Trustees hoped to build a lucrative silk trade in Georgia.

Perhaps most important of all, the Trustees prohibited the import of hard liquor and slaves into the colony. The prohibition of slaves doomed the colony to economic hardships for the next two decades. No one can fault the Trustees with insincerity; their intentions were good. However, without slaves, the colonists simply couldn't produce enough food and raw goods to balance the necessities they imported in order to survive. Other colonies didn't have this restriction and prospered quickly by exploiting their fellow humans. Without slaves, Georgia found it difficult to compete for newly arriving settlers and continued financing.

# James Edward Oglethorpe

Without Oglethorpe, U.S. history might be different. His vision and benevolence forced Georgia into reality. Later, his tenacity and cunning kept Georgia from falling to the Spanish. Had any other man stood between the colonies and Spain in 1742, Georgia might have fallen to the Spanish invaders. Most likely, the Spanish wouldn't have stopped there, but sailed on to Charles Town (Charleston). Under the Spanish, the American colonies might have rebelled earlier, later, or maybe not at all.

Oglethorpe was born into a wealthy English family on December 22, 1696. It was a turbulent time in a divided England. Royalists supported the recently crowned George I. Jacobites wanted James II restored as king. Sir Theophilus Oglethorpe, James's father, was a knight and a good friend of James II. When William of Orange removed James II, the Oglethorpes remained loyal to the defeated monarch. Eventually, King William forgave the family for their indiscretion.

The young James Oglethorpe became Prince Eugene of Savoy's aide-de-camp. He served with Prince Eugene at the Battle of Belgrade, where the Prince defeated the Turks. James left military service at the age of twenty and eventually took over the daily running of his family's estate.

In 1722, Oglethorpe won a seat in Parliament, but he almost didn't serve. During a drunken brawl, a crowd closed in on him. Believing himself in danger, he drew his sword and killed a man. He spent five months in prison before a court cleared him of murder. In October of the same year, a humbler Oglethorpe finally took his seat in the House of Commons.

As a member of Parliament, he formed the Prison Discipline Committee, which investigated prison corruption and implemented reforms. As chairman, he insisted committee members tour the prisons personally. It was during such a visit that he found his friend Robert Castell.

After Oglethorpe's American adventure, he returned to England and served in Parliament for thirty-two years. Quietly, from England's side of the ocean, he supported the American colonists in their war for independence. In June of 1785, Oglethorpe paid his respects to John Adams, the United States of America's first ambassador to England. Within days of meeting Adams, Oglethorpe died, on June 30, 1785.

When James Oglethorpe and Colonel William Bull designed Savannah, they planned many city squares around which houses would be built. A statue of Oglethorpe (above) was erected in one of those squares in 1910. The square is located on Bull Street.

Chapter

## Georgia's Promise Becomes Reality

On November 17, 1732, the *Ann* (also spelled *Anne* in some sources) left the port of Gravesend and sailed down the Thames River toward the English Channel. Perhaps some of the colonists on board stopped at the grave of Pocahontas, the famous Indian diplomat from Jamestown, Virginia, before boarding.

Among the group was an upholsterer, a printer, a gardener, a silk expert, a carpenter, a surveyor, a smith, a tailor, a wigmaker, a baker, a writer, a farmer, a stocking maker, an apothecary, and others. Also on board were wives and children—about twenty young children and babies and a dozen teens. The colony would have all the skills and labor required to build and sustain a colony.

Despite the Trustees' original philanthropic intentions, few of London's debtors made it to Georgia. In fact, during the twenty years that the Trustees were in charge, only twelve debtors made the trip to Georgia. The colony's success was more important than the debtor problem, and most debtors just weren't of good enough character and ambition for Georgia.[1]

While not debtors, most of the early settlers were poor—artisans, craftsmen, and laborers. The colonists received free passage, fifty acres of land, and all the supplies they would need for a year.

The passengers shared space with livestock and supplies. They slept as a group and enjoyed little privacy. Their meals consisted of salted pork, carrots, potatoes, stale bread, and beer. When able, the men fished from the ocean. Although they might have been bored with their rations, they didn't go hungry. Fresh water was precious and the crew carefully rationed what they had. Only two passengers died at sea—both were infants.[2] Four babies were born during the voyage.

After two months at sea, the colonists sailed into Charles Town, South Carolina, on January 13, 1733. South Carolinians settled the passengers in a barracks at Port Royal and Beaufort. Oglethorpe and Colonel William Bull of South Carolina headed for Georgia to find a site for Georgia's first English settlement.

The small party made their way south via an inland waterway to the Savannah River. Then they traveled northwest. Mile after mile, Oglethorpe's boat glided across the still water under huge pines that blocked the sky. The land was quiet as Oglethorpe watched the myrtle-draped shore pass by. The air was crisp and smelled of pine. Georgia was nothing like England.

As they rounded a bend in the river, a huge bluff loomed to the left. The party stopped and climbed the steep, forty-foot bank. Cresting the top of it, they could see a flat meadow all the way to the horizon. Atop Yamacraw Bluff, as everyone called it, the men turned to face a magnificent view of the river. It was the perfect site for Georgia's first settlement. The bluff would provide protection from a water assault. The river was deep enough for large ships to travel inland, making it easy to get people and supplies in and out of the settlement.

Oglethorpe already knew of Yamacraw Bluff by reputation. It was one of England's oldest trading posts. An English Ranger (a frontier soldier) named John Musgrove lived in the area and traded with the native peoples.

The Yamacraw Indians (who were part of the Creek nation) claimed the area where Oglethorpe and his colonists hoped to build their new settlement. Cherokee lived farther inland, but they often made hunting trips all the way to the Georgia coast. Chickasaws and Choctaws (allies to the French) lived farther west, near the Mississippi River. A small tribe known as the Uchees lived further inland along the Savannah River. South of the bluff lived the Upper Creeks and the Lower Creeks.

All of these tribes seemed to be continually at war with one another. However, the Creek and the Cherokee were less hostile to the settlers. They lived similarly to the colonists in that they grew crops and lived in permanent towns.

A tense truce existed between the area's natives and the South Carolinians, who promised the Indians that they wouldn't settle south of the Savannah River without the Indians' consent. Oglethorpe meant to honor that agreement and decided to meet with the Creek Indians through Musgrove.

Not far away, the exploration party found Musgrove's trading post, which was just a clearing with a few huts. Mary Musgrove, John's wife, met the white men. Mary, who was half Yamacraw Indian, arranged a meeting with Tomochichi, the Yamacraw chief. She interpreted so that the two men could negotiate.

Tomochichi presented a regal picture. He stood over six feet tall in his buckskin boots, breechcloth, and leggings. Otter skins adorned his neck, and his chest was bare. Other than a thin braid that hung over his left ear, his head was cleanly shaved.

Oglethorpe was impressed by the chief's generous reception. Tomochichi gave permission to settle the bluff area and even offered to help. He was eager to ally his people with the English against their common enemies, the Spanish and the French.

With Tomochichi's permission and gifts from the people of Charles Town—rice, hogs, cattle, horses, and various household items—Georgia's English settlers arrived at Yamacraw Bluff on February 1, 1733. Immediately, the settlers began to clear the foundation of Savannah, Georgia. Tomochichi, his wife, and John Musgrove paid a visit to welcome the settlers and to offer their help.[3] Another man danced with feather fans to show friendship. Bells hung from the feather fans, and they jingled as the man danced. It was an auspicious beginning for the inhabitants of the bluff.

Tomochichi was the chief of the Yamacraw tribe of Creek Indians. He was quick to ally with the English as their enemies were the same as his— the French and the Spanish. The boy is Tomochichi's nephew and heir, Toonahowi.

Tomochichi agreed to furnish fresh game so that the settlers could put most of their efforts into clearing land, building houses, and constructing a fence around the settlement.[4] Some tilled the soil. All the men took turns standing guard. The colonists weren't worried about natives; the Spanish were Savannah's biggest threat.

By the end of March, two houses were complete and more were in the works. The first houses were the same size, just twenty-four feet by sixteen feet. The settlers used timber for the walls and wood shingles for the roof. The ground floor had three rooms, and the occupants slept in a second-story loft.[5]

Together, Oglethorpe and Colonel Bull designed a town of several public squares. In fact, Oglethorpe was probably one of the first colonists to implement a city plan in the English colonies.[6] Each square created a small park, which citizens and visitors still enjoy today.

Between each square would be public buildings and markets. They named Savannah's main street Bull Street—after Colonel Bull.

Settlers found the differences between London and their new home startling. They had no luxuries and often went without necessities. The work of providing food and shelter was backbreaking. Even the smallest children worked.

The winter weather was milder than that of London's, but after a pleasant spring, they found the Georgia summer stifling. Through the insects and heat they persisted. Their only respite was an occasional thunderstorm, and those were far more violent than any they'd experienced in London. Many settlers fell ill, but they recovered quickly.

The Trustees expected the colonists to grow their own food, and eventually to grow enough for export to England. They also instructed the colonists to grow grapes for wine and mulberry trees to promote a colonial silk industry. Both wine and silk would take a substantial time investment, so it was clear that the Trustees were serious about their intentions. The Trustees even sent a botanist to Portugal's Madeira Island and the West Indies to gather plants and seeds for a public garden at Savannah.

Joseph Fitzwalter was in charge of the public garden, which they laid out along the Savannah River. They planted fruit, olive, and mulberry trees among the native magnolias. A kitchen garden provided grains, rice, beans, peas, and corn. Exotic plants, such as coffee, figs, and coconuts, made their way into the garden. Fitzwalter also grew cotton from seeds sent from Guinea. Despite the best intentions, the garden required too much time, and eventually the settlers abandoned it. However, it wasn't a total loss. From this garden came the original peach trees and cotton that later became major Georgia crops.

Savannah's settlers were better at maintaining good relations with the Indians than they were at growing crops. There were a few isolated Indian raids against Georgia settlers, but Oglethorpe and Tomochichi never broke their peace.

In July, Oglethorpe delegated many of his duties to a few hand-picked and trusted officials. He divided the town into wards, swore in a few bailiffs, and held the first session of magistrates.

**19**

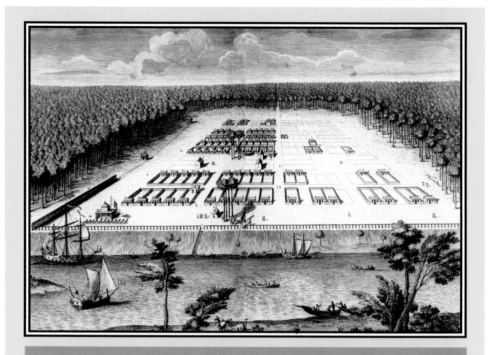

*The settlers followed a city plan created by James Oglethorpe and Colonel William Bull. Several public squares divided houses and shops. Those squares still exist in modern-day Savannah.*

Historians disagree on whether Oglethorpe was a good adminis-trator, although no one faults his sincerity or his motives. A few colonists died and several ran away to South Carolina. Those who remained survived fires, rain, stifling heat, insects, and illness. Still, they were 130-strong and they were working their own land. They were better off in Georgia than they had been in England.

## Georgia's Climate and Early Industry

Savannah, Georgia, lies at thirty-two degrees latitude, along with Jerusalem, Cairo, Baghdad, San Diego, and Dallas. The climate is subtropical, with hot summers and mild winters. Average temperatures range from the mid 30s to the high 90s. The annual precipitation is 110 inches. London lies farther north at about fifty-two degrees latitude, as do the Aleutian Islands off the southern coast of Alaska and central Newfoundland, Canada. London's climate is milder and drier than Savannah's.

Adjusting to the climate differences was difficult. Most settlers fell ill shortly after arriving, but recovered quickly. They came to call this period of illness "seasoning."

**Queen Caroline**

Although the Trustees considered the climate when planning the colony, things didn't go as they'd hoped. Silkworms don't like Georgia's unpredictable spring weather, and silk was a labor-intensive crop. Eventually, the colony did export silk to England. In fact, Oglethorpe sent thirty yards of Georgia silk to Queen Caroline. The best year, 1762, Georgians reeled over a thousand pounds of raw silk. By 1770, the colony was exporting very little silk.

Another disappointment was the hoped-for wine industry, which never did take hold. Georgia's soil and climate weren't suitable for wine grapes. Wild grapes were abundant throughout the colony, but they weren't suited for cultivation or winemaking.

Many colonists gave up on farming communal gardens and turned to raising cattle. Cattle provided a good income and food supply. However, with little law in the land, the livestock tempted the colony's criminal element. Owners branded their cattle, but the cows grazed freely in the woods and open meadows. Cattle rustling began in colonial Georgia, not the Wild West. Rustlers would steal the cattle, and, using creative designs, simply position a new brand over the original.

During the first few decades, Georgians tried to provide for themselves, but the colonists continued to lean heavily on the charter for provisions. They never were successful at producing raw goods to export to England—at least not to a degree that truly benefited England in an economic way.

In 1730, the Debatable Lands included Georgia. The Spanish weren't pleased when the English moved in, and eventually the two powers went to war. In the end, Spain surrendered Florida to the English.

Chapter

# 3

## Georgia, the Buffer Colony

Despite the English settlement in Georgia, the Spanish continued to refuse to concede its claim to the Debatable Lands. As the English settled into their new home, the Spanish strengthened their military forces in Florida. Spies kept an eye on the settlement's progress. Only a stronger British military presence, to the south of Savannah, would deter the Spanish.

With a southern fortress in mind, Oglethorpe made an expedition south in early 1733. He took Rangers and a couple of Yamacraw guides. The explorers traveled southward along the costal islands.

They floated through the salt marshes of Georgia's coast, suffering through hot afternoons, freezing nights, and the biting winds that blew inland from the ocean. Despite the hardships, they soon traveled past the Altamaha River and onto St. Simons Island. Just past the island, Oglethorpe spotted a high bluff and decided it was a good defensible spot.

Early in March 1734, a group of Austrian Protestants arrived at Savannah. Austria was hostile to Protestants, and Oglethorpe was sympathetic to their plight. On the practical side, he hoped to expand the colony, so he welcomed the Protestants to Georgia.[1] Eventually, the Austrians traveled inland and settled Ebenezer and then New Ebenezer.

Armed with maps of the coastal islands and plans for expansion, Oglethorpe, Tomochichi, and a few other Yamacraws sailed for London. Expansion would require money. Oglethorpe left Thomas Causton, a bailiff, in charge of the community and its forty houses, courthouse, and store. Smaller villages beyond Savannah also prospered: Highgate, Thunderbolt, Abercorn, Ebenezer, and Fort Argyle.

London welcomed Oglethorpe and his Yamacraw guests. Even King George II and Queen Caroline received Tomochichi and his wife. Beneath their borrowed robes, the chief and his wife wore buckskins and moccasins.

The Yamacraws were immensely popular in England. Their presence was a great public relations event and earned the colony plenty of positive publicity. Oglethorpe had succeeded on that count. What he hadn't expected was the cool reception he got from the Trustees. While in Georgia, he had done a poor job of keeping the Trustees informed, and now he was paying the price for his neglect.

Olgethorpe remained in London for a year and a half. (Tomochichi returned home without him.) During that time, he mended fences and spoke to the House of Commons on Georgia's behalf. Specifically, he wanted to enforce the prohibition on hard liquor and slaves, set down by the Trustees. The Trustees' restrictions had little impact in the American wilderness, and traders smuggled liquor and slaves into Georgia. Unless Parliament put some power behind the prohibition, it was useless.

In the end, Oglethorpe was successful, and Parliament ratified the prohibition. Liquor and slaves in Georgia weren't just an unenforceable restriction anymore. Their prohibition in Georgia was now English law. Parliament also ratified Oglethorpe's treaty with the Creeks.

His position on slavery put him at odds with almost everybody—both in England and in the American colonies. His ideals were controversial for the times. Prohibiting slavery was especially troublesome because the slave trade was a profitable business for England.

Many of his views would prove difficult to maintain over the next several years—but he never wavered on the issues of slavery or hard liquor.

To add to his Parliamentary victory, the Trustees gave him money to expand the colony. The colony's founding was a triumph, as far as King George II and the Trustees were concerned. Now the challenge was to protect it. To that end, Oglethorpe recruited 130 Scottish Highlanders, known for their courage and fierceness in battle, to settle along the Altamaha River.

During the year and a half Oglethorpe spent in London, over four hundred settlers moved to Savannah. Unfortunately, Causton, the bailiff whom Oglethorpe left in charge, had been a miserable administrator. Not only was he a bailiff, but he was the storekeeper. In Oglethorpe's absence, he used food and supplies to force the settlers to comply with his demands. Causton introduced stocks and a whipping post for corporal punishment. He was a dictator, not a leader. (The Trustees removed Causton for mismanagement in 1738.)

Oglethorpe returned to a troubled Savannah. Unfortunately for the citizens of Savannah, he didn't stay long and apparently didn't notice any conflicts. The Trustees blamed setbacks on the settlers. They believed some settlers were unworthy or just plain lazy.[2]

On February 14, 1736, Oglethorpe set out with a small party for St. Simons Island, again leaving Causton in charge of Savannah. They arrived four days later after a rough trip down river. Immediately, they began to build the fort's first shelters and defenses. Frederica, named for the Prince of Wales, was set on high ground overlooking the Altamaha River and acres of salt marshes. It was just south of the colony's original border and became Georgia's southernmost settlement.

Forty-four men and seventy-two women and children settled Frederica. Each man received a 60-by-90-foot lot for his house and family garden. The settlers dug wells, grazed cattle, and tended a public garden as well as their own. It took less than a month to complete the fort's walls. Near the north corner, which overlooked the river, they mounted cannons.

Wild game and grapes were plentiful on the island. Fresh fish and shellfish were abundant. The island was still a rugged and often fearsome place to live. Settlers dealt with hot weather, incessant rain, biting insects, alligators, and poisonous snakes. Despite the hardships, Frederica became an industrious settlement.

The Yamacraws supported the new settlement, which would also serve as a fortress for them. Oglethorpe and Tomochichi shared a common enemy—the Spanish. In fact, Tomochichi encouraged Oglethorpe to continue moving south. The farther south the English settled, the safer the Yamacraws would be. Oglethorpe continued to explore southward and claimed several islands for the English crown and Georgia: Jekyll, Highlands, Cumberland, Amelia, and St. George.

About this time, Oglethorpe and the Spanish governor of St. Augustine, Don Francisco del Moral y Sanchez, began to negotiate their common boundary. At first, Sanchez made gestures of peace and asked Oglethorpe to intercede on his behalf in convincing the natives to stop raiding Florida. Tomochichi knew that the Spanish settlement had been stocking guns and gunpowder. He wasn't convinced that Sanchez was sincere, but he agreed to keep his men north of the St. Johns River, the boundary between the Debatable Lands and Spanish Florida.

Months later, Oglethorpe received Sanchez's secretary off the coast of St. Simons Island. Highlanders, manning the ship, presented a menacing force. They stood tall in their tartans, with their ancient swords and shields at their sides. After toasting the King of Spain, Philip V, the ship fired a cannon salute. That signal echoed up and down the coast, and the English forts that dotted the islands answered in kind. It was clear to the Spanish secretary that the English were firmly entrenched in the Debatable Lands.[3]

Sanchez was quick to sign a treaty that agreed to settle all boundary disputes peacefully—back in the courts of Europe. Doing so sealed his fate and ended his career in Florida. The king recalled him, in disgrace.[4]

Despite a looming war over the Debatable Lands, the English Parliament called Oglethorpe home to answer to charges that he was mishandling the colony's money. South Carolinia traders continued to demand the right to sell liquor and slaves in Georgia. When they couldn't do so legally, they smuggled in both. Even with the new laws, Oglethorpe found it difficult to stop the smugglers.

**26**

*Sir Robert Walpole was England's prime minister. His goals didn't always match James Oglethorpe's. Walpole's demand that Oglethorpe disband his Georgia regiments was very unpopular with Georgians and the English. Eventually, Walpole had to rescind his order.*

The traders (and smugglers) saw Oglethorpe as an obstacle to free trade with Georgia. They wanted him gone. These jealous men made serious charges against Oglethorpe, and London demanded answers.

In London, Oglethorpe successfully defended himself against the unfounded charges. In fact, Parliament sided with Oglethorpe and cracked down harder on unlicensed traders. Parliament insisted that the South Carolinians deal with licensed traders only, hoping to put an end to the smuggling.

Defending his southern fortresses to the Trustees was a tougher battle. The Spanish ambassador to England, Don Tomás Geraldino, had complained about Frederica to the Parliament. When Oglethorpe defended the southern settlements, Spain ordered more reinforcements to St. Augustine. To avoid war, Prime Minister Sir Robert Walpole ordered Oglethorpe to disband his Georgia regiments. He hoped to convince Spain that England wasn't contemplating war over the Debatable Lands.

Oglethorpe was livid. The Georgians were his responsibility, and now Walpole was asking him to abandon them. Left defenseless, the Spanish would murder them all, he told Walpole. He refused to abandon them. Eventually, the prime minister gave Oglethorpe permission to recruit six hundred more soldiers from the king's infantry.

Despite the prime minister's reversal, the king and the Trustees insisted that Oglethorpe maintain peaceful relations with the Spanish. In addition, the Trustees reclaimed the administration of all civil matters in the Georgia territory. Publicly embarrassed by the demotion, Oglethorpe returned to Georgia as general of all British troops in South Carolina and Georgia, but he returned a military leader only.

In Georgia, the six hundred soldiers and their families settled into their new homes at Frederica. Meanwhile, Oglethorpe had a new problem. While he was in England, the Spanish incited South Carolina slaves to escape to Florida. The South Carolinians demanded that General Oglethorpe do something—he must find and return their property. The Spanish, of course, politely refused to help.

To add to Oglethorpe's personal burden, Tomochichi died. His loss was a heavy blow to Oglethorpe. The two men had been more than allies, they had become trusted friends. According to the chief's wishes, his people carried his body to Savannah, where he received a Christian funeral. Oglethorpe served as a pallbearer and openly wept with his Indian friends.

## The Scottish Highlanders

After spending two years in Georgia overseeing the administration of the new colony, Oglethorpe returned to England. One of his goals was to recruit soldiers, with the Trustees' permission. The English settlers weren't good soldiers. Consequently, defending the colony was difficult. Oglethorpe needed fierce warriors, not just farmers and shoemakers.

Oglethorpe hired Hugh Mackay and George Dunbar to travel to the Scottish Highlands. There, the two men recruited Highlanders, mostly from around Iverness, to serve as settler-soldiers. For protecting Georgia, they would receive land.

**Highlanders lay down their swords**

Highlanders had a reputation for being fierce and skillful in battle. Some even called them barbarians for their guerrilla-like tactics. They wore colorful plaid tartans and kilts and were experts with knives, which they used as weapons. Most importantly, they were a brave and robust people who could more than meet the challenge of defending the colonists in Georgia's wilderness.

On January 10, 1736, the Highlanders (men, women, children, and servants) disembarked at Georgia's southern border, the Altamaha River. Initially, they called the settlement New Iverness (now Darien). They chose a spot twenty miles northwest from St. Simons and just ten miles north of Frederica on a twenty-foot-high bluff surrounded by woods.

Hugh Mackay proved a worthy leader. By mid-February, the Highlanders, under Mackay's leadership, had completed a fort, a guardhouse, a storehouse, a chapel, and several small huts. While the Highlanders built their fort, a troop of Rangers from Savannah protected them. By mid-spring, the Highlanders were working on a second fort at St. Andrews.

Despite their rugged character, the Highlanders had a difficult time. The Spanish constantly raided their forts, and the sandy soil was hard to cultivate. Within a few years, they found raising cattle more prosperous than crop farming.

During the early years of the Georgia colony, most of the Highlanders remained loyal to Oglethorpe. They and their families bore more than their share of the war with Spain. In fact, without the Highlanders, Oglethorpe might have lost Georgia during the Spanish invasion of 1742.[5]

**FYI**

**For Your Information**

*From its fort in St. Augustine, Florida, Spain launched a war against Georgia and the other English colonies. It didn't work, and Spain lost its Florida territory as a consequence of losing that war.*

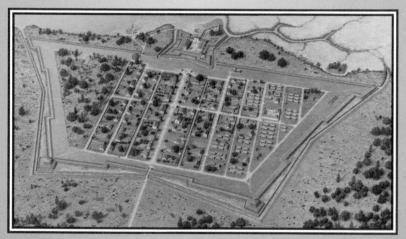

*Thanks to the small fort at Frederica, James Oglethorpe's forces, consisting of Georgia militia, the Scottish Highlanders, and Yamacraw Indians, were able to outwit the Spanish invaders.*

Chapter

# 4

## Georgia Faces the Spanish Alone

Hostilities between Spain and England grew. British merchants smuggled goods into Florida and the West Indies, despite restrictions bound by treaty. In return, the Spanish seized British ships and tortured English sailors. During one of these skirmishes, a Spanish sailor assaulted a British smuggler and cut off his ear. While slicing, the Spaniard shouted that he wanted to do the same to the king of England.

The earless Captain Robert Jenkins returned to England and demanded war. By showing his preserved ear while retelling his misadventure, he quickly turned popular opinion against the Spanish. Historians have only Captain Jenkins' word that the Spanish actually chopped off his ear, but the English believed him. While Prime Minister Walpole was trying to keep the peace with Spain, Jenkins had the common people of England clamoring for war.

Walpole, trying to appease the Spanish, agreed to withdraw all of Georgia's settlers and traders. In return, Spain agreed to pay reparations. Walpole was prepared to sell Georgia to keep the peace with the Spanish.

The deal was immensely unpopular. Several Trustees resigned in protest. In the end, Walpole succumbed to pressure and declared war on Spain. King George's War, as it was called in America, lasted for nine years.

Only Oglethorpe stood between Spain and the English colonies to the north of St. Augustine. For his part, Oglethorpe had no intentions of sitting in Georgia and waiting for the Spanish to arrive. He decided to attack St. Augustine.

The British fleet was unable to penetrate Spain's armada as planned. Upon arriving, Oglethorpe was disappointed to find St. Augustine well prepared for battle. A land assault was useless. After thirty-eight days, the Georgians retreated.

Oglethorpe requested more money to better train and equip his troops. At the same time, Thomas Stephens was in London, charging Oglethorpe with incompetence. Stephens represented a group of over one hundred citizens of Savannah who wanted to buy liquor and slaves. They also wanted absolute ownership of the land they worked. Stephens maliciously slandered Oglethorpe, and some believed his lies.

Parliament investigated Stephens' claims and found the Trustees and Oglethorpe innocent of all charges. Not only did Parliament clear Oglethorpe of all the charges, they commended the Trustees for their work. Stephens was publicly humiliated when forced to appear before Parliament on his knees to receive a reprimand.

Then, the worst happened. France and Spain joined forces against England. Europe was at war. England would need all its military resources on the continent. Georgia would have to face Spain alone.

With reports that the Spanish were about to attack St. Simons Island, Oglethorpe appealed to South Carolina for help, but the governor didn't even respond. Oglethorpe began to fortify Frederica, which seemed their best defense against a Spanish attack.

Georgians spotted a fleet of over fifty (some sources say around thirty) Spanish ships on June 28, 1742. Seven hundred Georgians waited at Frederica while the enemy landed and hacked their way through the island's jungle-like terrain. Fort St. Simons fell quickly.[1] The British garrison evacuated and retreated to Fort Frederica before the Spanish arrived on June 22.

Eventually the Spanish found Military Road, a thin strip cut through the forest to connect Fort Simons and Fort Frederica. The road was too narrow to accommodate heavy guns, but the troops adapted and advanced toward Fort Frederica via the old road.

General Oglethorpe led his troops straight down the road to meet the advancing enemy. With several hundred feet separating the two armies, Oglethorpe's forces disappeared into the dense forests on either side of the road. In a surprise ambush, the Georgians took the Spanish leader prisoner and the Spanish retreated—temporarily.

At this point, the Georgians had to keep the Spanish from reaching Frederica. In the woods, they had a fighting chance. The Spaniards outnumbered the Georgians, and in man-to-man combat at the fort, the Georgians would surely lose.

Oglethorpe sent the Highlanders and Yamacraw warriors back into the woods. While the Highlanders and Indians waited to ambush the Spanish a second time, Oglethorpe rode back to Frederica to warn the citizens, who had to be prepared if the Spanish approached Frederica by river.

The Spanish had other ideas. After retreating a bit, they stopped to rest in an open and unprotected area. They lit fires and began to cook, showing no fear that the Georgian troops might return at any moment.

Without waiting for Oglethorpe to return, the Highlanders and Indians slowly advanced toward the clearing, moving unseen and unheard from tree to tree. Finally in place, the Highlanders and Indians dashed out of the woods, attacking the Spanish as they ate. The Scotsmen used bayonets and the Indians threw tomahawks into the surprised faces of the Spanish.

The Spanish finally recovered from their shock and started shooting wildly. It began to rain. The smoke and rain obscured everyone's vision, and the Georgians dispersed into the woods, where they plotted another ambush. The Spanish troops assumed, incorrectly, that the Georgians had returned to Frederica and that the battle was over. They stacked their guns and once again lit fires to prepare a meal. The Highlanders and Indians again attacked from the woods. On July 7, in what became known as the Battle of Bloody Marsh, the Georgians slaughtered the Spanish.

Surprise and ambush served the Georgians well that day, and in truth, it was their only advantage. They couldn't have faced the Spaniards in open battle.

The Spanish were on the run. The Georgians followed, hoping to attack during the night when most of the Spanish would be asleep. Once the Georgians were within earshot, a mercenary fired a shot to warn the Spanish just before he deserted to the Spanish side.

Meanwhile, Oglethorpe had returned after warning the settlement and quickly withdrew his men to contemplate this unfortunate turn. The spy would surely confide all their weaknesses to the Spanish. Not even a surprise ambush would work to their advantage now. Oglethorpe did the only thing he could—he resorted to subterfuge.

Following Oglethorpe's orders, a few Georgians quietly approached one of their Spanish prisoners. In return for his freedom, would he carry a letter to the defecting spy? The letter was a bit of military genius. In that letter, Oglethorpe directed the spy to delay the Spanish until the British fleet arrived. The letter implicated the spy as a counterspy, in true alliance with the British![2]

The Spanish prisoner agreed, but after rejoining the Spanish troops, he turned the letter over to his commander, just as Oglethorpe had hoped. The effect was total confusion at the Spanish camp. Could their spy really be a British spy? As the Spanish argued over what to do, they spotted a few British ships sailing southward down the coast. The timing was a coincidence, as they weren't coming to Oglethorpe's aid, but the Spanish didn't know that. The Spanish thought the British fleet had arrived, just as promised in Oglethorpe's letter. The Spanish returned to their ships and sailed south on July 15. South Carolina troops finally arrived—after the Spanish were gone.[3]

With no help from England or South Carolina, Georgia had held its own against the Spanish. Physical strength and weapons hadn't stopped the invaders. The Georgians outmaneuvered them with their cunning trickery. In saving Georgia, the Georgians most likely saved all the English colonies in America.

Spain continued to threaten Georgia sporadically until the Spanish surrendered Florida in 1763. However, never again did they invade the Debatable Lands.

# Frederica: Fort and Town

*Fort Frederica Monument*

Oglethorpe founded Fort Frederica to defend the fledgling colony of Georgia. The site was sixty miles south of Savannah. The Spanish were just seventy-five miles south of the fort. Fort Frederica became the new colony's military headquarters.

The original settlement was both fort and town and consisted of forty acres, surrounded with an earthen wall (called a rampart). Beyond the wall was a dry moat and then two ten-foot-tall wooden walls (called palisades). The wall measured one mile in circumference. The fort location on a bend in the Frederica River allowed guards to spot enemy ships traveling toward Savannah.

The fort included three bastions, two storehouses, a guardhouse, and a stockade. At first, the settlers lived in small shelters called palmetto bowers. These were temporary structures made of branches and covered with palmetto leaves. Eventually the town resembled an English village. A central roadway called Broad Street separated lots. Each colonist had a 60-by-90-foot lot.

By 1743, nearly 1,000 people lived at Frederica. Unfortunately, peace was Fort Frederica's enemy. After King George's War, the post was unnecessary. The garrison disbanded and, subsequently, the settlement failed. Without any military presence, the settlement had no income or future. A fire in 1758 destroyed the few homes that remained. No one rebuilt at Fort Frederica, and time and the elements reclaimed the bluff.

Fort Frederica may have failed as a settlement, but its defense against the Spanish in 1742 was hugely successful. It was clear that the British held a powerful position in the southeast. In addition to Fort Frederica, the Georgia settlers established four more outposts. One was at the south end of St. Simons Island. Two were on Cumberland Island, one at the north end, one at the south. A fourth was on the St. Johns River in Florida.

In 1936, the federal government named Fort Frederica a national monument. Archaeologists began investigating the site in 1947. Using old maps and journals, they dug up sections of the fort and the town.

FYI

For Your Information

*James Oglethorpe returned to England after several years in Georgia. He never made it back to America, but lived for several decades at his English ancestral home at Godalming.*

Chapter

# 5

## Post-Invasion Georgia

After the Spanish failed to invade and reclaim Georgia, the colony slowly continued to grow. In a 1741 report to the Trustees, Georgia had 1,400 settlers (not including the soldiers). Savannah had 142 homes. Ships sailed up river as far as Augusta. Small forts dotted the coastal islands all the way to Cumberland Island. The town of Ebenezer built an orphanage in 1738. By 1740, both Ebenezer and Frederica had churches. By the time Savannah got its first dedicated church in 1744, Oglethorpe was home in England. He never returned to the colony.

The majority of Georgians were planters, but the colony also had merchants, shopkeepers, shoemakers, bricklayers, and common laborers. There were a few craftsmen, such as tailors and blacksmiths. Eventually, sawmills were added to the mix. Georgia was full of pine trees, and milling lumber became one of Georgia's largest industries.

Georgians struggled to make do in the colony without slaves. Indentured servants didn't take well to the backbreaking work, and they often ran away to South Carolina. Many settlers left Georgia and moved to other colonies, where they could use slave labor. Begrudgingly, the Trustees finally legalized the importation of slaves in 1749. They

*James Oglethorpe established a small fort on Cumberland Island. In fact, he founded several small outposts on the islands that dot the Georgia coast.*

had lifted the prohibition on liquor a few years earlier, in 1742. They also eventually bowed to the settlers' demands and allowed full ownership of the land. Soon after, in 1752, the Trustees gave up the Georgia charter altogether.

On October 29, 1754, Savannah received her first royal governor, John Reynolds. In 1755, Georgians held their first General Assembly. This was Georgia's first experience with a representative government. Their first law was to define punishment for anyone questioning their decisions. The real power remained with the governor, who had the authority to dissolve the General Assembly. Despite the drawbacks, it was a place to begin.

The Church of England was the colony's established church, but not everyone attended services. Lutherans, Presbyterians, Quakers, and Baptists also called Georgia home. Indians freely mingled with the settlers and often came to the towns.

Still, Georgia was a harsh place, like all the colonies. Everyone but the wealthiest worked hard. Children tended the gardens, fetched wood, and carried water. Women cooked meals in huge fireplaces and tended their private gardens. Men farmed, raised cattle, and served in militias.

With the French and Indian War raging, Governor Reynolds increased the militia to protect the settlers. His intentions in this area

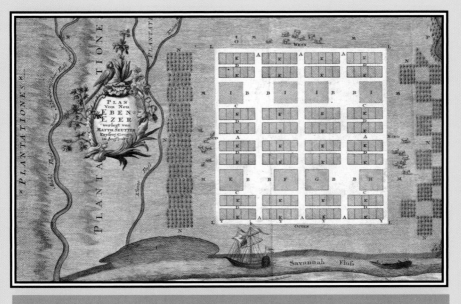

*The plan for the city of New Ebenezer was drawn in 1747. Protestants from Austria, called the Salzburgers, settled Ebenezer. Even though they were industrious and hard working, they couldn't succeed at that location. After six years, they moved to New Ebenezer.*

were probably good ones, but he wasn't an effectual governor.[1] When he couldn't get the General Assembly to do what he wanted, he dissolved it, instead of negotiating. In 1757, the king recalled Reynolds to England.

Georgia's next governor, Henry Ellis, was a better choice. Both Georgians and Indians found him amiable, sincere, and hardworking. He left Georgia in 1760 when he became ill.

Under Governor James Wright, Georgia finally began to prosper in earnest. The conclusion of the French and Indian War in 1763 provided the security Georgia needed. Unfortunately, the treaty reduced Georgia's western boundary, which had stretched all the way to the Pacific Ocean. The border would now be the Mississippi River. On the other hand, Spain surrendered Florida to England, and Georgia extended her southern border all the way to the St. Mary's River. The Debatable Lands were truly no longer in debate. Settlers from all over

*Governor James Wright was a loyalist who supported the English Crown and the unpopular Stamp Act. His views put him in conflict with the citizens of Georgia.*

America poured into Georgia and the colony flourished—at least until the British passed the Stamp Act.

The French and Indian War had cost England dearly. King George III meant to recover that debt from the American colonists. After all, in the king's mind, he was protecting the colonists, and they should pay for that protection.

The Stamp Act required a stamp on all legal documents—and there was a fee for that stamp. Georgians protested the new law, as did the other American colonists.

Governor Wright was a royally appointed official, and his loyalties remained with the British. Twice, rebellious Georgians assaulted the governor; both times, he was able to disperse the challengers.

Still, England and not Georgians paid Governor Wright. In addition, Georgia's colonists depended on England for trade and maintaining peace with the Indians. Breaking with England was a slow process for most Georgians.[2]

It wasn't until the British closed the port at Boston after the Boston Tea Party that Georgia's Patriots began to organize in a meaningful way. Like many colonists, Georgians met to discuss the situation in Boston and drew up a set of resolutions. However, they sent no delegates to the First Continental Congress, and sent only one delegate to the Second Continental Congress.

The battles at Lexington and Concord motivated Georgia's Liberty Boys, a well-organized gang of Patriots, to act. They stole the governor's gunpowder stores and incited a riot. Without troops or support from England, Governor Wright was no longer in control of the colony—the Liberty Boys were.

Rebel law became Georgia law, and the law was harsh. The gang retaliated quickly and violently against their opponents. Their favorite revenge was to tar and feather their enemy—any citizen who opposed war with England.

Later that year, three Georgians signed the Declaration of Independence: George Walton, Button Gwinnett, and Lyman Hall (who was the only Georgian to attend the Second Continental Congress). Georgians, along with colonists all over America, celebrated their independence. Georgia's rebel-elected president, Archibald Bulloch, read the Declaration of Independence to the large crowd that had gathered. They fired cannons, made toasts, and even held a mock funeral for King George III. With great fanfare, Georgians buried the king in effigy. In his patriotic speech, Bulloch said:

> . . . let us remember America is free and independent;
> that she is, and will be, with the blessing of the Almighty,
> great among the nations of the earth. Let this encourage
> us in well-doing, to fight for our rights and privileges,
> our wives and children, for all that is near and dear unto
> us. . . .[3]

**41**

## The Coastal South in the Revolutionary War

Despite the efforts of Georgia's Liberty Boys, Savannah fell to the British in December 1778. On July 22, 1779, James Wright, the royal governor, returned to Savannah and reestablished British control. In October that year, Patriots tried to liberate Savannah, but they were unsuccessful.

**Nancy Hart attacks soldiers**

Georgians looked to the other colonies for help, but none came. Patriots held only a small part of the state in the northwest corner. During this time, the story of Nancy Hart, a Georgian living in the back-woods, came to light. When six British soldiers appeared on her doorstep and demanded food, she prepared a tasty feast. They stacked their weapons and sat down to eat. Nancy seized one of their guns and held them at gunpoint until Patriots in the area came for them.

Although the story is legend, supporters insist that a 1912 article in the *Atlanta Constitution* mentioned the discovery of six skeletons on property owned by Nancy Hart. No known copy of this article exists.[4]

In May 1780, the British captured South Carolina's garrison and Charles Town fell. Independence for the southern states looked grim. That fall, a backwoods militia clashed with 1,200 British troops at King's Mountain, South Carolina. The British, trapped on an open plateau, were easy targets for the Patriots. It was the bloodiest battle since Bunker Hill: 225 British soldiers died, 163 were wounded, 716 were taken prisoner; only 28 Patriots died and 68 were wounded.

Many historians consider this battle the turning point of the war. News of the battle encouraged Patriots to continue the fight. Guerrillas under the leadership of Thomas Sumter, Andrew Pickens, and Francis Marion (the Swamp Fox) worked with the Continental Army to chase Lord Cornwallis into Virginia, where he surrendered to George Washington on October 19, 1781.

From Yorktown, General Anthony Wayne took five hundred men south to free Savannah. After five months of skirmishing, the British withdrew to Charles Town and Florida. Lt. Col. James Jackson reclaimed Savannah for Georgians, and Wayne headed for Charles Town. Jackson eventually chased British troops south. He was at Skidaway Island on July 25, 1782, at the last battle between American and British troops in Georgia.

# Chapter Notes

## Chapter 1
### The Promise of Georgia
1. Coleman, Kenneth. *Colonial Georgia: A History* (New York: Charles Scribner's Sons, 1976), pp. 13–14.
2. Jackson, Harvey H., and Phinizy Spalding (editors). *Forty Years of Diversity* (Athens: The University of Georgia Press, 1984), p. 49.
3. Ibid., p. 52.
4. Ibid.

## Chapter 2
### Georgia's Promise Becomes Reality
1. Saye, Albert Berry. "Was Georgia a Debtor Colony?" *The Georgia Historical Quarterly*, December 1940, Vol. 24, No. 4, p. 330.
2. Coleman, Kenneth. *Colonial Georgia: A History* (New York: Charles Scribner's Sons, 1976), p. 24.
3. Ibid., p. 32.
4. Ibid., p. 30.
5. Ibid.
6. Ibid., p. 29.

## Chapter 3
### Georgia, The Buffer Colony
1. Coleman, Kenneth. *Colonial Georgia: A History* (New York: Charles Scribner's Sons, 1976), p. 43.

2. Jackson, Harvey H., and Phinizy Spalding (editors). *Forty Years of Diversity* (Athens: The University of Georgia Press, 1984), p. 55.
3. Coleman, pp. 56–57.
4. Ibid., p. 57.
5. Ibid., pp. 49–50.

## Chapter 4
### Georgia Faces the Spanish Alone
1. Coleman, Kenneth. *Colonial Georgia: A History* (New York: Charles Scribner's Sons, 1976), p. 70.
2. Ibid., p. 71.
3. Ibid., p. 72.

## Chapter 5
### Post-Invasion Georgia
1. Jackson, Harvey H., and Phinizy Spalding (editors). *Forty Years of Diversity* (Athens: The University of Georgia Press, 1984), p. 254.
2. Coleman, Kenneth. *Colonial Georgia: A History* (New York: Charles Scribner's Sons, 1976), p. 270.
3. White, George. *Historical Collections of Georgia* (New York: Pudney & Russell, Publishers, 1854), p. 201.
4. Cobb, James C. *Georgia Odyssey* (Athens: The University of Georgia Press, 1997), pp. 7–9.

# Chronology

**1717** Sir Robert Montgomery publishes *A Discourse Concerning the Designed Establishment of a New Colony to the South of Carolina, in the Most Delightful Country of the Universe.*

**1721** Colonel John Barnwell of South Carolina builds the first British settlement in the Debatable Lands, Fort King George, but it fails.

**1729** Seven of the Lord Proprietors surrender their rights to the Carolina territory to George II.

**1730** On July 30, James Oglethorpe and twenty associates petition George II for a royal charter to establish a new colony south of South Carolina.

**1732** On January 27, the Privy Council approves the requested charter for lands between the Savannah and Altamaha Rivers from the Atlantic coast to the south sea for twenty-one years.
On July 20, the original twelve trustees attend the first meeting of the Trustees.

**1733** On January 13, the *Ann* arrives in Charles Town, South Carolina, with the first Georgia colonists. The next day, the *Ann* heads for Port Royal; Oglethorpe and his first exploration party leave for Georgia. On February 1, the colonists reach Yamacraw Bluff, which will become Savannah, Georgia. On July 7, Oglethorpe calls together the first Georgian court.
On October 18, the Creek-Oglethorpe treaty is ratified.

**1734** On March 12, a group of Protestants from Austria, the Salzburgers, arrive in Savannah. In June, Oglethorpe arrives in England with Tomochichi, his wife, and other Indians.

**1736** On February 6, Oglethorpe returns from England.
Late in the year, Oglethorpe returns to England.

**1739** In October, England declares war on Spain (War of Jenkins' Ear, also known as King George's War).

**1740** On January 1, Georgians, led by Oglethorpe, head for Florida. In June, Oglethorpe's troops spend three weeks trying to penetrate St. Augustine's defenses. In July, Oglethorpe's men retreat.

**1742** On July 7, Georgians meet the Spanish at the Battle of Bloody Marsh. Parliament repeals the law prohibiting hard liquor in Georgia.

**1743** On July 11, William Stephens becomes president of Georgia.

**1744** Oglethorpe returns to England, never to return to Georgia.

**1749** Parliament repeals the law prohibiting slaves in Georgia.

**1752** On June 23, the Trustees officially surrender their charter.

**1754** On October 31, Georgia's first royal governor, John Reynolds, takes his oath of office.

**1755** On January 7, Georgia's first Assembly meets at Savannah.

**1757** Governor Henry Ellis arrives and relieves John Reynolds of duty, by order of Parliament.

**44**

| 1760 | James Wright becomes governor of Georgia. |
| 1763 | The colony's first newspaper, the *Georgia Gazette*, begins publication. |
| 1769 | Jonathan Bryan convinces citizens of Savannah to boycott British goods. |
| 1775 | Habersham raids Savannah's royal magazine. |
| 1778 | On December 29, the British occupy Savannah. |
| 1779 | On January 29, Augusta is captured by the British. |
| 1785 | The University of Georgia is chartered; it is the first state university in the U.S. |
| 1788 | Georgia is the fourth state to ratify the Constitution. |

# Timeline in History

| 1663 | Charles II grants the Carolina territory to the lords proprietors. |
| 1665 | Charles II extends the Carolina territory to just south of St. Augustine, claiming Georgia territory for the English—at least according to the English. |
| 1670 | English settle Charles Town, South Carolina. Spain concedes all existing English settlements in the Debatable Lands as English territory in Treaty of Madrid. |
| 1673 | Spanish build stone fort at St. Augustine. |
| 1680s | Spanish retreat south from the Debatable Lands when Yuchi, Creek, and Cherokee Indians ally with the English. |
| 1702 | South Carolinians, under Governor James Moore, invade Florida and capture St. Augustine, but are unable to seize the fort, pushing Spanish frontier from St. Mary's River to the St. Johns River. |
| 1730 | Parliament passes the Debtors Act to protect debtors. |
| 1754 | The French and Indian War begins in North America. |
| 1760 | George II dies; George III takes the throne. |
| 1763 | The French and Indian War ends; the Spanish surrender Florida to the British. |
| 1765 | Parliament passes the Stamp Act. |
| 1766 | Parliament repeals the Stamp Act. |
| 1773 | Patriots in Massachusetts hold the Boston Tea Party. |
| 1774 | Patriots hold the First Continental Congress in Philadelphia, in September. |
| 1775 | On April 19, American Patriots meet British forces at Lexington and Concord. On May 10, Patriots meet for the Second Continental Congress. On June 15, the Continental Congress appoints George Washington as commander in chief of the Continental Army. |
| 1776 | The Continental Congress approves the Declaration of Independence. |
| 1781 | Cornwallis surrenders at Yorktown. |
| 1783 | Treaty of Paris is signed; the U.S. Constitution is drafted. |
| 1785 | James Oglethorpe dies. |

# Further Reading

## For Young Adults

Bartley, Numan V. *The Creation of Modern Georgia*. Athens: The University of Georgia Press, 1983.

Blackburn, Joyce. *James Edward Oglethorpe*. Philadelphia: J. B. Lippincott Company, 1970.

Brown, Ira L. *The Georgia Colony*. Springfield, OH: Crowell-Collier Press, 1970.

Clements, John. *Georgia Facts: A Comprehensive Look at Georgia Today, County by County*. Dallas, TX: Clements Research II, Inc., 1989.

Draper, Lyman C. *Kings Mountain and Its Heroes: History of the Battle of Kings Mountain*. Baltimore: Genealogical Publishing Company, 1967.

Duncan, Russell. *Freedom's Shore*. Athens: The University of Georgia Press, 1986.

Garrison, Webb. *Oglethorpe's Folly: The Birth of Georgia*. Lakemont, GA: Copple House Books, 1982.

## Works Consulted

Bonomi, Patricia U. *Under the Cope of Heaven: Religion, Society, and Politics in Colonial America*. New York: Oxford University Press, 1986.

Boorstin, Daniel J., and Brooks Mather Kelley. *A History of the United States*. Upper Saddle River, NJ: Pearson Education, Inc., 2005.

Bridenbaugh, Carl. *The Colonial Craftsman*. New York: New York University Press, 1950.

Cobb, James C. *Georgia Odyssey*. Athens: The University of Georgia Press, 1997.

Coleman, Kenneth. *Colonial Georgia*. New York: Charles Scribener's Sons, 1976.

Gallay, Alan. *The Formation of a Planter Elite*. Athens: The University of Georgia Press, 1989.

Jackson, Harvey H. and Phinizy Spalding. *Forty Years of Diversity: Essays on Colonial Georgia*. Athens: The University of Georgia Press, 1984.

Saunt, Claudio. *A New Order of Things: Property, Power, and the Transformation of the Creek Indians, 1733–1816*. New York: Cambridge University Press, 1999.

Saye, Albert Berry. "Was Georgia a Debtor Colony?" *The Georgia Historical Quarterly*, Vol. 24, No. 4, December 1940.

## On the Internet

The Avalon Project at Yale Law School, "Georgia Charter: 1732"
**http://www.yale.edu/lawweb/ avalon/states/ga01.htm**

Colonial America 1600–1775
**http://falcon.jmu.edu/~ramseyil/ colonial.htm**

Georgia Historical Society
**http://www.georgiahistory.com/**

Georgia History
**http://www.cviog.uga.edu/Projects/ gainfo/gahist.htm**

National Park Service: Fort Frederica
**http://www.nps.gov/fofr/**

New Georgia Encyclopedia
**http://www.georgiaencyclopedia. org**

Our Georgia History
**http://www.ourgeorgiahistory.com**

# Glossary

**abominable**
**(ah-BAH-mih-nah-bul)**
Detestable or loathsome.

**altruistic**
**(al-troo-IS-tik)**
Promoting and doing good works for no personal gain and for no reason other than the results of the deed.

**armada**
**(ar-MAH-duh)**
A fleet of warships.

**bankrupt**
**(BANG-krupt)**
Totally lacking funds or means of paying off debts.

**bastion**
**(BAS-chun)**
Part of a well-fortified wall that protrudes from the protective wall.

**bayonet**
**(BAY-uh-net)**
A blade that fits into the muzzle of a rifle and is used as a weapon in close combat.

**boycott**
**(BOY-kot)**
To refuse to buy or support a particular product or brand.

**catalyst**
**(KAA-tuh-list)**
A component that sparks an action or response.

**coup**
**(KOO)**
A win or an advantage.

**creditor**
**(KREH-dih-tur)**
Someone who lends money to another.

**Jacobite**
**(JAY-kuh-byt)**
A supporter of James II of England.

**myrtle**
**(MER-tul)**
A bushy evergreen that flowers.

**panacea**
**(pah-nah-SEE-uh)**
A remedy for all diseases or difficulties; a cure-all.

**palisade**
**(PAH-lih-sayd)**
A wooden wall or fence made of stakes set upright and usually chopped to a sharp point at the top.

**Patriot**
**(PAY-tree-ut)**
A colonist who wanted American independence.

**philanthropic**
**(fih-len-THRAH-pik)**
Providing humanitarian or charitable help.

**plight**
**(PLYT)**
An especially bad or unfortunate situation.

**respite**
**(REH-spit)**
A short interval of rest.

**smallpox**
**(SMALL-poks)**
A serious disease that killed or permanently scarred many of the colonists.

**subterfuge**
**(SUB-ter-fyooj)**
Deceptive strategy.

**surmise**
**(ser-MYZ)**
To guess or draw a conclusion.

# Index

**48**